PEBBLES

Poems and Writings of Spiritual Inspiration

Eleanor Streicher Faber

Aaron Press
Naperville, Illinois

Library of Congress Control Number: 2008933185

ISBN 978-0-9795656-1-8

Acknowledgments

Scripture taken from the New King James Version ®. Copyright © 1982 by Thomas Nelson, Inc. Used by permission. All rights reserved.

Images and photos:

© 2007 Jupiterimages Corporation: cover, 3, 11, 13-15, 18, 26-28, 32-34, 37, 38, 40-42, 44-46, 49, 51-60, 63, 65-67, 70, 71, 75, 78-87, 89-92, 94-100, 102, 103, 105, 107-116, 119, 121-127, 130, 132, 134, 136-139, 166; Bible and cross: 5, 13-138, 141.

© 1995-2001 Nova Development Corporation: 5, 9, 16, 17, 19, 21-24, 29-31, 35, 39, 43, 47, 48, 61-62, 64, 68, 69, 74, 88, 101, 104, 106, 131, 133.

© 1989-1995 C.A.R., Inc.: 20, 36, 50, 77, 93, 118, 120, 128, 62.

© 1994 Zedcor, Inc.: 25, 117, 134, 67.

© 1995 Zedcor, Inc.: 47, 72, 76.

To my daughter, Janet Faber Crawford, for all her help and encouragement that led these words to print. With her insight, talent and research, she devoted countless hours matching my writings with appropriate pictures.

With love and gratitude,
Mom

Contents

Introduction 7

Writings of Eleanor Streicher Faber 9

Scripture References 141

Index

Writings of Eleanor Streicher Faber...169

Scripture References 172

ABOUT THE AUTHOR

In August of 1972, Eleanor Streicher Faber received a spiritual calling relating to Karma. Karma means kingdom attainable through righteous management of actions.

Galatians 6:7-9 (Scripture Reference page 148)

Seven years later, she was inspired to open a prayer room to share her thoughts and ideas about life and living. Soon after, her first writing came to her: "All of work, life, and living is a means to an end of understanding our oneness with the creative spirit, God".

Since then, she has received many more writings from thoughts and visions that life is a journey of being, becoming one with the light.

Eleanor Streicher Faber, mother of five children, grandmother of eleven, lives in Oak Park with her husband Bob.

INTRODUCTION

Pebbles was written under the inspiration and guidance of the Holy Spirit, some writings came from thought, others from visions. The title of the book, *Pebbles*, came to me in a vision, an altered state of consciousness. I saw the ocean rolling in, and along the shoreline were pebbles. On the right they were bright and shiny, and as I looked left they were less and less shiny reaching a point of total dullness. In this altered state the words came:

The tide comes in, and the tide goes out,
The tide comes in, and the tide goes out.

Each one of us is a pebble on the grains of
    sand in the ocean of life.

And the tide comes in, and the tide goes out,
    for the purpose of cleansing and purifying
    us until we shine as the morning star.

Eleanor Streicher Faber

WRITINGS OF
ELEANOR STREICHER FABER

OPENING PRAYER

Dear Lord, Our God, we come to you for courage and strength to carry out our daily responsibilities.

We ask that you give us the assurance that everything is working together for good when we follow God's plan, even though at times life seems difficult.

Help us to realize that in order to know joy, we must know sorrow, to know strength we must know weakness, and to know love, we must know hate.

Let us know that life and living and all experiences are necessary for our spiritual growth, and they are part of eating of the tree of life.

Help us to be kind and forgiving with ourselves, as we are kind and forgiving with others.

Teach us to respect and help one another, knowing that respect brings peace into our lives, and with peace comes joy, and on the wings of joy comes happiness, and when we're happy, we have health of both body and mind.

Help us to understand that we are all growing toward the imaging of our Creator, God, and sometimes people that are close to us do not have the same level of understanding as we have.

Help us to tolerate these conditions knowing that through prayer and faith our answers will come bringing with them another learning experience.

We know your help and answers are on the way as we now go into the silence to make our communion with our Lord within.

Amen

ACCEPTANCE

God will feed you
as long as you are willing to be fed.

Matthew 6:26

ACQUIESCENCE

Accept
Christ
Quietly
Understanding (that the)
Indwelling
Eternal
Spirit (is)
Cradling (the)
Entity (and)
Nurturing (its)
Character (into the)
Expression (of GOD).

I John 5:20

AFFIRMATION

Affirming (that only through)
Feelings (will I)
Find (the)
Invisible
Redeemer (who is the)
Master (and)
Almighty
Tutor (of wisdom),
Instructing
On (the)
Nature (of balancing feelings
   and wisdom, thus becoming
   alive in Christ).

Ezekiel 11:19-20

<u>ANGELS' WINGS</u>

Life is a journey,
life is an
adventure, and life
is sometimes
painful. But when
you hear the flutter
of the angels'
wings your
thoughts will be
uplifted, and then
you shall be
uplifted.

Psalms 57:1

AN APPLE

What is this red round thing we call an apple? This delicious fruit that will multiply itself many times over if allowed to drop to the ground. Are we like the apple with seeds of thought that will grow and manifest into form if we allow it to be? To be God's creator; that is the way it was meant to be.

Zechariah 8:12

ATTRACTION

Attune (your)
Thinking
Toward
Right (God)
Activity, (thus)
Centering (your)
Thoughts (that will)
Initiate (the)
One
Natural (God power
      into Action).

II Samuel 22:33

BALANCE

There is an unchangeable balance in the Universe; as you sow, so shall you reap. This is known as cause and effect or the law of Karma.

Galatians 6:7-9

<u>BE FLEXIBLE</u>

Bending
Everyday (through)

Faith
Lessens
Encasement (and)
X'es (out)
Inhibitive
Behavior (so the)
Lamb (of God can)
Express (freely and fully).

Hebrews 11:1

THE BEACON

God is my beacon morning, noon, and night,
Turning his beam in the tower that holds his light,
Guiding and directing me on the playground of
  life,
Encouraging and watching and freeing from fear,
The next adventure with lessons that will bring me
  nearer to thee,
Honesty, love and compassion must be felt in the
  heart,
Dispelling deception and darkness and bringing to
  light that God is my Beacon, my Savior and
  Friend,
My playmate in life as I gradually ascend.

I John 1:5-7

BEHIND CLOSED DOORS

She sat in a chair,
A chair with wheels that is,
And gazed out the window
To see the birds flying
With the freedom of a gentle breeze.
A long time it has been
Since she has known such a feeling.
Deeper into her thinking she began to fly
Like the birds in a gentle breeze,
And the feeling returned,
Only this time deeper and higher.
She ascended above the clouds
Into an atmosphere of Spirit knowing,
No longer a prisoner in her mind,
But a free spirit into the knowing mind of God.

John 8:31-32

Be (aware of all)
Opposing
Negative (thought forces that)
Disagree (with)
Almighty
God's
Eternal (truth for you: love, happiness,
      health, peace, joy and prosperity).

Romans 8:2

BOW AND ARROW

What the bow is to the arrow,
The Spirit is to the vessel.
What mind is to matter,
Sun is to earth.
What rain is to growth,
God is to us.

I Thessalonians 4:4

CABOOSE

Surely as the caboose follows the engine, our thoughts follow us.

Proverbs 16:3

CASKET—BASKET

Do not plant your hopes, desires, and strength in a
  casket of doubt and fear,
But plant them in a God given basket of rich soil,
  and watch your life flourish.

Psalm 92:12-13

THE CASTLE

Her hands moved surely and swiftly upward
  molding and shaping the mound of clay.
Near completion and coming into sight was a
  castle.
The top of the castle had three spires.
Atop each spire was a flag,
One green for nature, one blue for the sky, and
  one white for the beyond.
The lower part of the castle had many doorways
  for people to enter,
Some friendly, some not.
The upper part of the castle had many windows
  for ideas to enter,
Some beneficial, some not.
The inner part of the castle had one room with
  one door for special people to enter.
Angels above, help me guard the door well,
  for this is where my heart dwells.

Proverbs 4:23

<u>CELLAR OF ESCAPE</u>

Cellar of escape is using illicit drugs, drinking too much alcohol, sleeping too much, or eating too much.   All resulting from trying to push the off button emotionally on life.   In order to grow spiritually you must remain open, alive, and alert to all of life's situations, and in so doing you will grow ever closer to God, Love.

Luke 21:36

CENTER OF LIFE

I put God in the center of my life, He is my eye of
protection as I walk the path of life, guiding and
directing me in the storms of life, instructing and
telling me to put God and myself in the center, the
circle of my life. I will not hear God if I put another
in the center of my life. When I listen for guidance
the path of my life is lit with assurance as I follow
the light in the center of my life.

Exodus 20:1-3

CHILD OF GOD

I am a child of God; therefore, I am strong, I am happy, and I am healthy.

II Timothy 3:15

CHILDREN

If you had no time for your children when they were growing up, when grown your children will have no time for you.

II Corinthians 12:14

Veni Creator Spiritus
Mentes tuorum visita
Imple superna gratia
Quæ tu creasti pectora
Accende lumen sensibus
Mentes tuorum visita
Infirma nostri corporis
Virtute firmans perpetim

<u>CHISEL</u>

You are the chisel in your life. Use it with wisdom,
and your dream castle will appear on the wings of
the angels from above.

James 3:17-18
Carving Translation - page 167

COMFORTER

Call
Openly (on your)
Master (Lord within)
For
Order (in your life)
Regarding
Trials, (and you shall be)
Engaged (in)
Revelations, (thus living productively).

John 14:17-18

CREATIVE

Constructive (thoughts)
Render (to the)
Eternal (God)
Action, (thus directing us)
Toward
Inventive (ideas which will bring the)
Veritable
Energy (forces into being for positive results.)

Ephesians 2:10

CREATIVE SPIRIT

All of work, life, and living is a means to an end of understanding our oneness with the Creative Spirit, God.

II Thessalonians 3:10

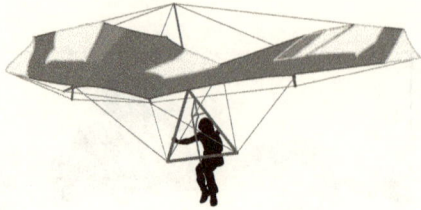

CREATOR

The more creative I am in a God given way,
  the happier I am;
The happier I am, the healthier I am;
The healthier I am, the more productive I am;
The more productive I am, the closer to God I am;
The closer to God I am, the more I image my
  Creator, God.

Genesis 1:26-27

DECEPTION

When we are sure of ourselves in a righteous way we have no need to set traps of deception for anyone.

II Timothy 2:18-19

<u>DEMONSTRATE</u>

Demonstrate (the)
Eternal
Master's
Omniscient
Nature, (and)
Steadfastly
Trust (the Lord)
Regardless (of)
Appearances (knowing that)
Through (faith the)
Everlasting (gifts of God will express).

James 2:17-18

<u>DESERT OF LIFE</u>

Lost in the
desert of life,
seeking the living
waters of the
kingdom.

Jeremiah 29:11-13

DIVINE MIND

Prepare your thoughts in order before you put your
order into the Divine Mind.

Philippians 2:5

THE DOOR

Standing by the door with past memories,
Conditioned and a creature of habit,
Wanting closeness but love and hate so near,
Reaching out but holding back,
Speaking but with no sound,
Trying and yet failing,
Fear too strong yet love so near,
Then with the inner ear,
Life and living became clear.

Proverbs 22:17
Revelation 3:20

FAITH

Love sustains us; faith carries us through.

II Thessalonians 1:3

<u>FATHER OF LIGHTS</u>

When I am troubled I will say, "Get thee behind me Satan." If I have to say it a dozen times I will until I see a way, a clearing.

The more I place my faith and trust in God the more liberated I will become. With this freedom I will gradually come to know that:

James 1:17 "Every good gift and every perfect gift is from above, and comes down from the Father of lights, with whom there is no variation or shadow of turning."

James 1:17

FEELINGS

A heart of flesh is a heart that feels;
A heart that feels knows before the words
  are revealed;
The words revealed comes from a heart
  concealed;
A heart concealed is revealed to a heart
  that feels.

Ezekiel 11:19-20

THE FOOL

What a fool I have been,
To trust the outer
  instead of the Spirit within,
To see with the eyes of a mortal
  rather than the eyes within,
To seek comfort from without
  rather than the spirit within,
To put others at the helm
  rather than the Spirit within,
To lower my eyes to the valleys
Rather than to the hills of the Spirit within.

Proverbs 18:2

FRAGILE

Fragile is the human mind
Like the early mist on a newborn bud.
Fragile are the thoughts of the mortal mind
Like the opening of a newborn bud.
Powerful is the mind of Spirit
Open to the power of the morning sun.
Powerful is the torch of love
Open to the morning sun.
Beautiful is the sturdy bloom
Resulting from the power of faith in the
  newborn sun.

Hosea 14:5

FREEDOM

Freedom is to be able to fly like a bird in the sky of life or to swim like a fish in the ocean of life.

Revelation 21:6

<u>FURNACE OF LIFE</u>

The man was big and burly with an intent
  look on his face,
Kindness in his eyes and a pulsating purpose
  in his heart;
To his right a furnace, door open and flames
  visible,
In his hand an iron rod which he extended
  into the flames,
He removed the rod; it was bright red with
  intense heat,
He set the rod down on an anvil that was in
  front of him,
In his left hand he held a felt covered mallet,
He raised the mallet high above his head and
  with all his might came down hard on the rod,
He rested and repeated the action six more
  times, resting in between each blow which
  numbered seven in all,
After the seventh blow the rod was free from
  all heat and color, displaying a perfectly
  shaped heart,
Mission accomplished, a heart full of feeling
  revealing the light and love of God.

Deuteronomy 4:20

FUTURE

Let go of the past; look to the future.

Song of Solomon 2:11

GARDEN OF CHOICE

I am a garden unto myself;
I sow, I water, I cultivate, and I reap.
I am the gardener, and I will reap
  exactly what I sow.

Isaiah 58:11

<u>GATES</u>

Lying and hypocrisy will keep the gates to the kingdom closed. Love, Honesty and Compassion will open them.

Psalm 118:19

GENERATOR

When the lights go out, call on
God your generator.

Gods
Eternal
Natural
Energy
Retrieves
All (confusion and)
Turns (chaos into)
Order (thus)
Redeeming (problems.)

I John 1:5

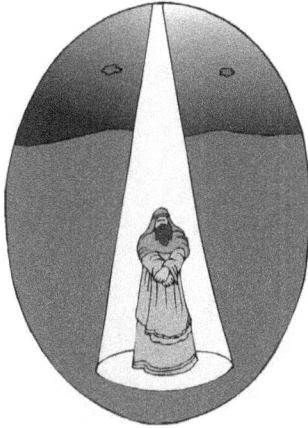

<u>GENESIS</u>

In the beginning God,
In the silence answers,
In answers guidance,
In guidance comes the way,
    the light, and the truth.

Psalm 18:30

<u>GOD</u>

Thank you God for helping me keep my life alive.

Deuteronomy 4:4

GOD IDEAS

God given ideas will light your path to positive results and bring into your life happiness, health, peace, joy, and prosperity.

I John 1:5

<u>GOD IS MY LIGHT</u>

Life is a progressive, evolutionary state of consciousness or self-awareness.

Honesty, love, and compassion must be felt in the heart, dispelling deception and darkness and bringing to light that God is my lamp in the darkness of night.

Psalms 18:28

CHRIST BLESSING THE LITTLE ONES

GOD'S CHILD

You are God's child, so claim heartily your inheritance, so you can live dynamically.

Romans 8:16
Psalm 16:5

GOD'S SANCTUARY

Go
Open-hearted (to your)
Divine
Spirit (within, and)

State
All (of your)
Needs.
Cast (your)
Tribulations
Unto (the)
All-(knowing)
Redeemer, God, (and)
You (will find your way).

Psalm 77:13

GOLDEN RULE—CREATIVE LOVE

Practicing the Golden Rule is Creative Love, a love that brings peace. With this peace comes happiness. This happiness produces a healthy mind that comes forth with individual beneficial God talents, talents that bring advancement and betterment to life and living. They bring to life and light that what benefits me benefits all in the name of Creative Love. This is all accomplished when we practice the Golden Rule.

Matthew 7:12

HALL OF JUSTICE

The day was peaceful, the sky inviting,
The fields abundant as the wheat moved in a sun
  lit breeze;
In the distance a building of marble statuesque and
  standing alone,
On approaching a sense of awe, beauty, and
  mystery pervaded me,
My eyes were raised upward and high above the
  gold-bordered doors were the words
                HALL OF JUSTICE,
The doors swung open inward, barren was
  the room,
The floor was marble, columns of the same,
Engraved in one column a snake, suddenly coming
  alive and slithering onto the floor,
In the upper right corner a crown of thorns,
  twelve in number,
My eyes were raised upward, words
                HALL OF JUSTICE,
Inner voice announcing, temptation no longer,
Upper right corner a crown of jewels, twelve in
  number,
Trumpets sounding, rays descending, spirit
  ascending to that heavenly place.

James 1:12

<u>HARDEN NOT YOUR HEART</u>

Awaken (to dead)
Works, (and)
Allow (the)
Redeeming,
Eternal,
Natural,
Everlasting
Spirit (within to)
Satisfy (the yearning
       of the heart).

Psalm 17:15

HEART OF FLESH

Hearken
Everyone
Always
Remember (the)
Truth (that)

Only (through)
Feelings (can you)

Find
Love, God, (and)
Establish
Spiritual
Happiness (which is
        wholeness).

Ezekiel 36:26

HOLY SPIRIT

It is an inward knowing, expressing in an outward manifestation of works, resulting from faith, hope, and love.

I Corinthians 2:10

HOUSE OR HOME

Possessions without love are nothing,
Love without sharing is empty,
Compassion feigned is tragic,
Confusion through trusting is blinding,
Then inner sight, a ray of sunshine,
A long journey back through faith brings hope,
Continued faith brings change,
Now my house is becoming my home,
I am the home.

II Corinthians 5:1-8

<u>I AM A CHILD OF GOD</u>

Therefore:
I will stand up straight,
I will throw my shoulders back,
I will hold my head up high,
And with the help of God
I will see my way clear to overcome obstacles.
I live, move, and have my being in the Spirit of God.

Amen

Exodus 3:14

IMPRESS—EXPRESS

I AM NOT HERE TO IMPRESS YOU
BUT TO EXPRESS ME.

I Corinthians 3:13-14

IN MEMORY

She stood by the water's edge,
Her mind flooding with past memories,
Her sensitivity soaring above the roaring of
  the waters on the edge,
Her heart dictating her emotional needs,
Memories from past lives to past lives,
Hurts giving way to the Divine Will,
Knowing that all her needs will be filled in
  time according to Divine Will.

Romans 2:7

INDIAN CHIEF

He stood in the middle in a line of twelve braves,
He looked regal among them in his headdress of
  twelve feathers,
Words of wisdom flowed from his heart to his eyes,
His words glistened as they met the rays from the
  morning sky.
"Take care of your temple, nourish it well,
For the living waters of the kingdom, dig deep into
  your well."

Proverbs 5:15

INTERNAL FLAME

The internal flame burns brighter and brighter until all negativity is consumed. Then the pure heart ascends becoming one with the morning star.

Judges 13:20

<u>INTUITION</u>

In (your)
Natural (being within exists)
The
Understanding (Savior who will)
Influence (you)
To (seek)
Inner (guidance)
Of (the Lord, thus)
Naming (God, the pilot of your vessel).

Psalm 51:6

<u>KARMA</u>

Kingdom
Attainable (through)
Righteous
Management (of)
Actions.

Acts 14:22

KATIE ON THE WRONG TRACK

Katie was trying to cope with life,
Young and good looking and neatly dressed,
Intelligent but fearful and wearing a mask,
Sensitive and moving but on the wrong track,
Alcohol clouding her brain, easing her pain,
  but still on the wrong track,
Playing the game in the big top of life,
With painted face and long bangs covering her
  beautiful but sad green eyes,
Sensitive to another one's pain,
I hugged her with love, and her soul was regained,
Her mask lifted, her eyes now bright,
She's on the right track, her journey has begun,
Trust and love have brought her back,
  the sure cure to bring anyone back.

II Timothy 2:19

KNOW THYSELF

SELF-
LOVE

SELF-
UNDER-
STANDING

SELFLESS

SELF-
DISCIPLINE

SELF-
PERSE-
VERANCE

SELF-
INTEREST

SELF-
RESPONSI-
BILITY

SELF -
RESPECT

SELF -
HONESTY

SELF-
CONFI-
DENCE

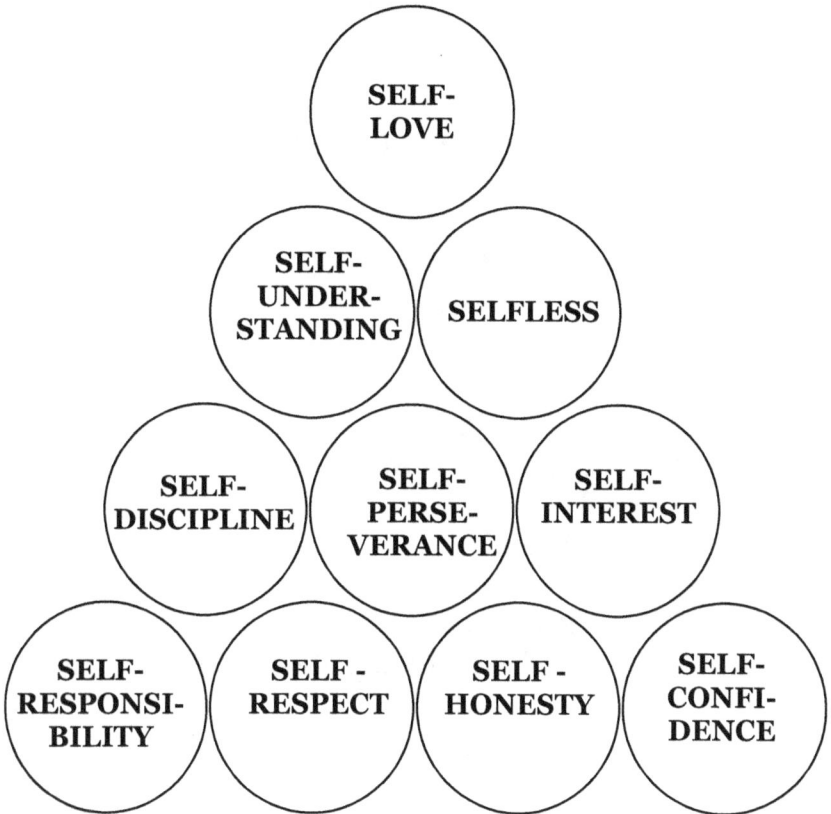

Philippians 4:8

LIFE IS A PARITY

Listen
Individuals
For (each)
Entity

Is (being)
Seasoned (toward)

Attaining

Perfection,
And (when complete will be)
Received
Into (the)
Temple (of)
Yahweh.

John 5:24

<u>LOVE</u>

I can't buy it,
I can't borrow it,
I can't steal it,
I grow into it,
And it manifests itself through me.

Matthew 22:36-40

MAGICAL POWER

What is this magical power we call love? Can we see it, can we hear it, can we touch it, can we taste it, can we feel it? Look at nature and see.

Song of Solomon 2:12
II Timothy 1:7

MIND OVER MATTER

Men and Women (have)
Inside (a)
Natural
Doctor (who)

Overcomes (illness of the)
Vessel.
Every
Responsive

Man and Woman (who pays)
Attention (to the)
Teacher (of)
Truth, God,
Ends (up)
Rejoicing (and healed).

Luke 5:17

<u>MY BODY</u>

My body is always listening to me and will perform for me exactly what I say to it. My body is always repeating to me what I have said to it.

Luke 11:34

<u>MYSELF</u>

Who knows me better than me?
Do I have the courage to look within me?
Because I give to others what is within me,
That is if I don't pretend to be.
If I express me, then what is meant for me will be.

II Corinthians 8:21

NAME OF LOVE

In the heart of my being is the core of <u>LOVE</u>,
Wanting to express in the name of <u>LOVE</u>,
Growing and unfolding being one with <u>LOVE</u>,
Creating and becoming in the name of <u>LOVE</u>,
What benefits me benefits all in the name of
 <u>CREATIVE LOVE</u>.

II Chronicles 31:21

NEW CREATION

Every success ripens into a new desire, and every new desire is open to a new creation.

Matthew 25:14-31

<u>NOTICE</u>

Love is caring,
Caring is noticing,
Noticing is awareness,
Awareness is recognizing the needs
  and the oneness of self and others,
Oneness is sharing our God-given gifts,
Bringing to light the allness and oneness
  of all of life.

I Corinthians 12:6

<u>ONENESS WITH GOD</u>

I declare and affirm my oneness with God,
My provider and teacher on the shores of life,
My strength and my tutor as I make my way in life,
Finding and becoming one with the light.

John 3:1-6

OPEN—ALIVE—ALERT

We cannot give to another what we have not developed within ourselves and only when the senses are open, alive, and alert can we develop.

Psalm 133

PEACE AND SUNSHINE

Don't fix the blame,
Put God at the rein,
And He will guide you out of the rain,
Into the lane of peace and sunshine.

I Thessalonians 5:23

<u>THE PEACE OF GOD</u>

Trust
Him (in)
Everything (regardless of the)

Picture
Earthly (eyes present, and)
Attune (your)
Consciousness (to the)
Eternal,

Omniscient
Father, (God, who will)

Guide (you into)
Order (and give you)
Dominion (over your life).

John 14:27-28

PEBBLE REPRESENTS GROWTH

The tide comes in, and the tide goes out,
The tide comes in, and the tide goes out.

Each one of us is a pebble on the grains of sand
in the ocean of life.

And the tide comes in, and the tide goes out for
the purpose of cleansing and purifying us until
we shine as the morning star.

   Purity, perfection (is your)
   Eternal (quest while being)
   Baptized (in the ocean of life to)
   Become (a shining)
   Light (in the world for the sake of the)
   Everlasting (inherent God Almighty, the
              morning star).

Revelation 22:16

<u>PILOT OF YOUR VESSEL</u>

Let the pilot of your vessel come forth and be known
unto you, and let it take you down the path to the
road of the way, the light, and the truth.

Psalm 119:105

POSITIVITY

Stand firm on the mountaintop of positivity; do not allow yourself to slip down into the valley of negativity.

I Thessalonians 3:8

THE PLATFORM

She stood alone on the wooden, weathered, oblong
 platform facing east with a feeling of dejection,
Clouds forming, matching her thoughts, darkening
 the sky,
Then clouds giving way to a ray of sunshine,
 piercing and opening the veiled light,
Her thoughts now lifted, her vision clearing,
Surrounding the platform throngs and throngs
 of people,
God's helpers, they were awaiting her
 acknowledging eye,
Then words of wisdom in her ear,
"How foolish you are to allow one person, one
 incident, one circumstance to ruin your life,"
To the right of the platform a hangman's noose,
Negative thoughts will choke out life, but you will
 not die,
To the left of the platform a red chair representing
 God's kingdom,
Now you can dwell on the negative or sit in the
 chair of the positive; the choice is yours,
God's inheritance is rightfully yours; trust, believe,
 and accept with the mind of a child.

Psalm 16:5

<u>PRAYER</u>

Planned
Righteous
Action
Yields
Eternal
Rewards

Psalm 58:11

<u>PRAYING</u>

Praying renews the mind, which actively yields to the eternal power within and resurrects the God knowledge into manifestation.

James 2:14

RAINBOW

Redeemed (through righteous)
Actions (the)
Invisible
Native (spirit within sees the rainbow
and accepts the)
Bountiful (gifts from the)
One (spirit God, resulting from)
Works (of pure love).

Psalm 84:11

<u>REACTION</u>

Remember
Every
Action (has a)
Corresponding (reaction)
That (will bring)
Into (your)
Objective (world either)
Negative (or positive results).

Romans 12:2

<u>REFLECTION</u>

My life is a reflection of my thoughts and ideas.
When I look in the mirror do I like what I see?
Am I bright and alive and eager to succeed?
Or downhearted and confused, unable to be?
Expecting from others what I should expect of me,
I am one of a kind, unique in all ways,
When I turn to the Light I will be able to see.

James 1:23

REMAIN OPEN

Remain open, alive, and alert to all of life's situations, and in so doing you will grow ever closer to God.

Psalm 119:18
Luke 24:45

REPLACE

With God's help I will replace negative thoughts with positive thoughts. With these thoughts, one at a time, I will build a stairway of sunshine to success.

Psalm 121

<u>REPLENISH</u>

I must replenish my physical and spiritual needs daily. In meditation I will give way to the Spirit of Truth within by saying, "Not my will but Thine will be done." In so doing God will show me the right way.

Psalm 1:1-3

REPLICA

I am a reproduction of the ETERNAL SPIRIT GOD, who places light into my consciousness. I accept the flow of good through righteous thinking. I plant GOD-given seeds in the field of life, and as I labor I reap the fruits of my thoughts. As I come into the realization of my oneness with the ETERNAL GOD POWER I can see the light of ascension.

Psalm 17:15

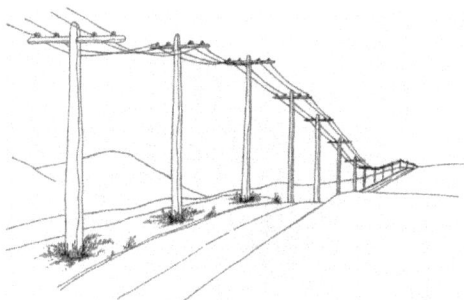

RESOURCE

God is your source, so continually call on your resource.

Rely (on the)
Eternal
Spirit (within to)
Open
Unto (you natural)
Resources (that will)
Care (for all your)
Earthly (and spiritual needs).

Luke 12:29-31

<u>RIGHT THINKING</u>

We are thought forces, and by right thinking we are
spiritually and physically healed.

Jeremiah 17:14

RIGHTEOUSNESS

Right
Intention (brings)
Godly
Harmony
To
Everyone (who is)
Open (to the)
Understanding
Spirit (within, who)
Nourishes
Equally (to all who)
Seek
Spiritual (guidance).

James 3:17-18

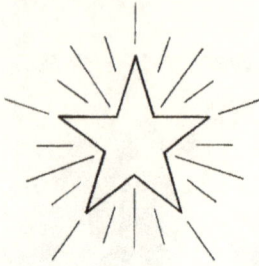

RIVER STONE

I am a river stone in the waters of life,
Being pushed ashore when the time is right,
Smooth and free from cracks and bumps,
From the many eons of the rushing waters
  in the turmoil of life,
Now on the shore, the morning star with
  its sunbeams so bright,
Gathered me up to shine, one with the light.

Psalm 36:9

ROSE OR CARNATION

In a meditative state I was trying to visualize a
   red rose.
I finally got my rose, but it was wax,
I shoved it aside and said "I want a real rose,"
In place of the rose came a carnation.
It was small, pink, and all the petals were tipped
   with white.
The word carnation stems from the word carnal,
   meaning flesh, and pink is the color of hope.
God, my Savior, is knocking at the door giving me
   hope, strength, and courage.
Now, I am using my God-given talents as I reach
   for the morning star.

I Corinthians 3:1-3
Titus 1:2

RUFFLED FEATHERS

Don't let anyone ruffle your feathers. You must be able to fly spiritually as you ascend higher and higher in thought until you are one with the morning star, no longer a spark of life but a spark of light.

Psalm 19:7-11

SEEDS

May the seeds of your thoughts blossom into beautiful reaping.

Isaiah 55:6-13

<u>SELF</u>

Seek (the)
Eternal
Life
Force (within for energy,
        wisdom, and guidance).

Job 5:8-11

SELF-DECEPTION

Self-deception is most harmful, and under these conditions we cannot be honest with ourselves or others.

Lamentations 3:39-41

SELF-EVALUATION

Steadily
Eliminate
Lingering
Fictitious (opinion of self and)

Elevate (your mind to the)
Veritable
Almighty
Lord's
Understanding (that the)
All (knowing)
Teacher (is)
Inviting (you to)
Openly (express his)
Nature (and goodness).

Philippians 2:1-6

SELF-PROJECTION

Seeing
Everything (in the)
Light (of)
Free (spirit, I will)

Prepare (the)
Road (as)
Only (I can do on my)
Journey
Establishing (rightness of)
Character
Towards (the)
Insight (of projecting the)
Oneness (of my divine)
Nature (with God, being totally free of
        hypocrisy as I ascend into the
        Light of the morning star).

Psalm 36:9

SENSIBILITY—SENSITIVITY

Sensibility-sensitivity is the ability to see behind the
screen, beyond the scene of life.

Revelation 22:1-5

SENSITIVITY

The sensitive part of individuals is their Soul. The primary function of the intellect is for Soul growth.

Ephesians 2:20-22

<u>SILENCE</u>

In the silence our Soul communicates with our conscious mind, and in so doing Body and Soul become one.

Philippians 2:5

SINCERITY

Sincerity (shows)
Itself
Naked (with no)
Covering; (thus, it is)
Empty (of)
Reproach; (therefore the)
Intuitive
Truth (can express through)
You (naming GOD Almighty
     your Lord and Master).

Ephesians 6:24

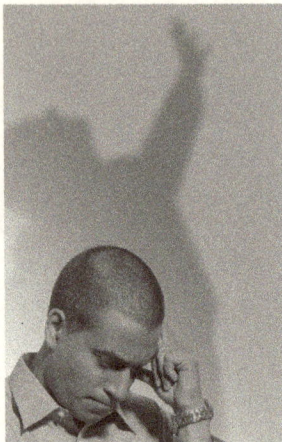

SOMETHING TOLD ME

Spirit within my Holy Master, give me entrance to intuitive ideas that will help me find my way.

I Corinthians 3:7-10

SOUL DISCOVERY

Self (is)
Only (the outer shell).
Underneath (is the)
Living,

Dynamic,
Intelligent, intuitive
Soul (waiting to)
Cast (its)
Omnipotent,
Veritable
Energy (on the waters of life, thus)
Revealing (the real)
You.

II Corinthians 4:15-18

<u>SOUL GROWTH</u>

In the process of Soul growth we begin to grow out of a selfish state into a selfless state, thereby helping and loving one another, not using and abusing each other.

Proverbs 17:17-18

SPARK OF LIFE

I am a spark of life, an atom of fire;
My veins are pulsating with courage
  and strength;
The journey is long, my energy is high,
My sights are steady, my bow is strong,
The arrow is ready, the timing is perfect,
My awareness is heightened to express,
The bull's-eye is bright, the target is met,
God given ideas in season are expressed.

Psalm 1:1-3

SPECTATOR AND DIRECTOR

Get out there on the stage of life and perform. God is your spectator, and God is your director.

Proverbs 3:6

SPIRIT OF TRUTH

When you give way to the Spirit of truth,
the Spirit of truth will make a way for you.

Psalm 18:30

STEP ASIDE

Spirit
Thinks (through my)
Entity (and)
Prepares (me for the)

Attainment (of)
Satisfying (my)
Indwelling (Spirit's)
Desire (to)
Enter (into the dominion of the
        righteousness of God).

Psalm 85:13

SUCCESS

Success (is)
Understanding (that the)
Creative
Christ (is in your)
Entity (and will)
Satisfy (all)
Spiritual (and earthly needs as you
        follow inner direction).

II Thessalonians 3:5

SUCCESS: CHANCE OR CHOICE

It isn't in the roll of the dice,
It isn't in the dealing of the cards,
It is in the choice of following the feeling
  of the heart.

John 10:27

SUMMER

Dawn is approaching as I walk along the shores of
  the Mediterranean Sea,
My senses come alive as I watch the sun making its
  appearance on the horizon,
The soft rhythmic waves touch on my hearing, and I
  am one with them,
The smell of the salt water in the air trickles down
  to my taste buds,
My senses fully awake and alive; I realize I am one
  with nature.

Psalm 74:17

TANDEM

Going with God is like working in tandem;
you get there twice as fast with half the effort.

Romans 8:28

<u>TEMPLE OF GOD</u>

Life is valuable, so listen carefully, for each entity is being seasoned toward attaining perfection and when complete will be received into the temple of God.

I Corinthians 6:19

<u>THOUGHTS</u>

Thoughts (are things and should be)
Handled (carefully as to which)
Ones (you want to manifest in your life,)
Understanding (that some bring about)
Good (results, while others can)
Hurt (and cause)
Trouble, (so)
Select (wisely).

Proverbs 1:5

THREE DROPS OF BLOOD

After scrubbing the kitchen floor I waited awhile
  before applying the wax.
Now dry I knelt on the pad, poured the wax
  and spread it around.
On my knees I began to ponder my life and was
  doing a lot of complaining to myself.
Suddenly from above three drops of blood fell into
  the wax.
Startled, I went into the bathroom to check my face,
  my nose, and my throat; there were no signs of
  blood.
I went back to the kneeling pad, and now the blood
  was mixing into the wax.
Then in thought the words came:
"You do not get there without suffering."

Romans 8:17 – And if children, then heirs—heirs of
God and joint heirs with Christ, if indeed we suffer with
Him, that we may also be glorified together.

Revelation 7:14 – And I said to him, "Sir, you know."
So he said to me, "These are the ones who come out of
the great tribulation, and washed their robes and made
them white in the blood of the Lamb."

TORCH OF LOVE

Your Christ will come like a torch in the night,
To guide and lead you to an upper flight,
A flight so high you can hardly bear,
To shout your joy so all can share,
So give of your knowledge of the light of love,
And the pitfalls of darkness when you shun
   the above,
It is up to you, you have a choice,
Whether you stumble in darkness or use
   God's advice.

Colossians 2:2-3

TRUST AND BELIEVE

Through many incarnations I come into the realization of my TRUE SELF, MY CHRIST, the KINGDOM WITHIN. I become aware of God's beneficial thoughts. Not my will but thine will be done. I feel an elevation when I least expect it. I come into knowing that everything has its season, and God has everything in perfect order. I move on my God-given ideas, and it brightens my day. The clouds disappear as I allow God's thoughts to move through me. I feel myself ascending and getting closer to Christ Consciousness.

Psalm 103:19

UNIFIED FOUR

God first, family second, job third,
and recreation fourth.
In this order, you will have order in your life.

I Corinthians 14:40

WINTER

Dusk is falling in and around me,
The sky darkens sending glistening
    snowflakes on my path,
I hear the crunching of the snow; it
  lightens my way,
As I look upward the flakes touch on my
  Lips, and I taste a little bit of heaven,
The path leads me to a small white
  steepled building,
On entering, the smell of incense announces
  the eve of the birth of the Messiah.

Isaiah 9:6

<u>WISDOM</u>

Wise
Instruction (from the Holy)
Spirit (brings)
Development (that)
Only (the)
Master (teacher of truth, God, can do.)

Proverbs 4:7

WITHIN

Within (every)
Individual (lies the)
Truth (of)
His or her (being, the)
Inherent
Natural (God ability to
      solve all problems).

Psalm 46:1

<u>WORK</u>

Wonders
Occur (when you take the)
Responsibility (to allow the)
Kingdom (of God to express
                through you).

Deuteronomy 3:24

YOU ARE GOD'S DIAMOND

Dazzling
Intuitive (power)
Aligns (your life as you)
Mount (and)
Overcome (all)
Negative (situations until your)
Diamond (shines as the morning star).

Revelation 22:16

<u>YOUR CONCEALED BEING</u>

Your concealed being, consciously becoming.

Philippians 1:27

IN CLOSING

GOD IS ALL

From east to west, to north and south,
  God is all,
From spring to summer, to fall and winter,
  God is all,
From dark to light, to sunset and sunrise,
  God is all,
From bad to good, to cold and hot,
  God is all,
From hate to love, to sorrow and happiness,
  God is all,
From my will, to God's will,
  God is all,
From struggling and suffering, to salvation,
  God is all.

SCRIPTURE REFERENCES

Acts 14:22 – Strengthening the souls of the disciples, exhorting them to continue in the faith, and saying, "We must through many tribulations enter the kingdom of God."

II Chronicles 31:21 – And in every work that he began in the service of the house of God, in the law and in the commandment, to seek his God, he did it with all his heart. So he prospered.

Colossians 2:2-3 – That their hearts may be encouraged, being knit together in love, and attaining to all riches of the full assurance of understanding, to the knowledge of the mystery of God, both of the Father and of Christ,
In whom are hidden all the treasures of wisdom and knowledge.

I Corinthians 2:10 – But God has revealed them to us through His Spirit. For the Spirit searches all things, yes, the deep things of God.

I Corinthians 3:1-3 – And I, brethren, could not speak to you as to spiritual people but as to carnal, as to babes in Christ.
I fed you with milk and not with solid food; for until now you were not able to receive it, and even now you are still not able;
For you are still carnal. For where there are envy, strife, and divisions among you, are you not carnal and behaving like mere men?

I Corinthians 3:7-10 – So then neither he who plants is anything, nor he who waters, but God who gives the increase.

Now he who plants and he who waters are one, and each one will receive his own reward according to his own labor.

For we are God's fellow workers; you are God's field, you are God's building.

According to the grace of God which was given to me, as a wise master builder I have laid the foundation, and another builds on it. But let each one take heed how he builds on it.

I Corinthians 3:13-14 – Each one's work will become clear; for the Day will declare it, because it will be revealed by fire; and the fire will test each one's work, of what sort it is.

If anyone's work which he has built on it endures, he will receive a reward.

I Corinthians 6:19 – Or do you not know that your body is the temple of the Holy Spirit who is in you, whom you have from God, and you are not your own?

I Corinthians 12:6 – And there are diversities of activities, but it is the same God who works all in all.

I Corinthians 14:40 – Let all things be done decently and in order.

II Corinthians 4:15-18 – For all things are for your sakes, that grace, having spread through the many, may cause thanksgiving to abound to the glory of God.

Therefore we do not lose heart. Even though our outward man is perishing, yet the inward man is being renewed day by day.

For our light affliction, which is but for a moment, is working for us a far more exceeding and eternal weight of glory,

While we do not look at the things which are seen, but at the things which are not seen. For the things which are seen are temporary, but the things which are not seen are eternal.

II Corinthians 5:1-8 – For we know that if our earthly house, this tent, is destroyed, we have a building from God, a house not made with hands, eternal in the heavens.

For in this we groan, earnestly desiring to be clothed with our habitation which is from heaven,

If indeed, having been clothed, we shall not be found naked.

For we who are in this tent groan, being burdened, not because we want to be unclothed, but further clothed, that mortality may be swallowed up by life.

Now He who has prepared us for this very thing is God, who also has given us the Spirit as a guarantee.

So we are always confident, knowing that while we are at home in the body we are absent from the Lord.

For we walk by faith, not by sight.

We are confident, yes, well pleased rather to be absent from the body and to be present with the Lord.

II Corinthians 8:21 – Providing honorable things, not only in the sight of the Lord, but also in the sight of men.

II Corinthians 12:14 – Now for the third time I am ready to come to you. And I will not be burdensome to you; for I do not seek yours, but you. For the children ought not to lay up for the parents, but the parents for the children.

Deuteronomy 3:24 – 'O Lord God, You have begun to show Your servant Your greatness and Your mighty hand, for what god is there in heaven or on earth who can do anything like Your works and Your mighty deeds?'

Deuteronomy 4:4 – "But you who held fast to the Lord your God are alive today, every one of you."

Deuteronomy 4:20 – "But the Lord hath taken you, and brought you forth out of the iron furnace, even out of Egypt, to be unto him a people of inheritance, as ye are this day."

Ephesians 2:10 – For we are His workmanship, created in Christ Jesus for good works, which God prepared beforehand that we should walk in them.

Ephesians 2:20-22 – Having been built on the foundation of the apostles and prophets, Jesus Christ Himself being the chief cornerstone,

In whom the whole building, being fitted together, grows into a holy temple in the Lord,
In whom you also are being built together for a dwelling place of God in the Spirit.

Ephesians 6:24 – Grace be with all those who love our Lord Jesus Christ in sincerity. Amen.

Exodus 3:14 – And God said to Moses, "I AM WHO I AM." And He said, "Thus you shall say to the children of Israel, 'I AM has sent me to you.'"

Exodus 20:1-3 – And God spoke all these words, saying:
"I am the LORD your God, who brought you out of the land of Egypt, out of the house of bondage.
"You shall have no other gods before Me."

Ezekiel 11:19-20 – "Then I will give them one heart, and I will put a new spirit within them, and take the stony heart out of their flesh, and give them a heart of flesh,
"That they may walk in My statutes and keep My judgments and do them; and they shall be My people, and I will be their God."

Ezekiel 36:26 – "I will give you a new heart and put a new spirit within you; I will take the heart of stone out of your flesh and give you a heart of flesh."

Galatians 6:7-9 – Do not be deceived, God is not mocked; for whatever a man sows, that he will also reap.

For he who sows to his flesh will of the flesh reap corruption, but he who sows to the Spirit will of the Spirit reap everlasting life.

And let us not grow weary while doing good, for in due season we shall reap if we do not lose heart.

Genesis 1:26-27 – Then God said, "Let Us make man in Our image, according to Our likeness; let them have dominion over the fish of the sea, over the birds of the air, and over the cattle, over all the earth and over every creeping thing that creeps on the earth."

So God created man in His own image; in the image of God He created him; male and female He created them.

Hebrews 11:1 – Now faith is the substance of things hoped for, the evidence of things not seen.

Hosea 14:5 – I will be like the dew to Israel; He shall grow like the lily, and lengthen his roots like Lebanon.

Isaiah 9:6 – For unto us a Child is born, unto us a Son is given; and the government will be upon His shoulder. And His name will be called Wonderful, Counselor, Mighty God, Everlasting Father, Prince of Peace.

Isaiah 55:6-13 – Seek the Lord while He may be found, call upon Him while He is near.

Let the wicked forsake his way, and the unrighteous man his thoughts; let him return to the Lord, and He will have mercy on him; and to our God, for He will abundantly pardon.

"For My thoughts are not your thoughts, nor are your ways My ways," says the Lord.

"For as the heavens are higher than the earth, so are My ways higher than your ways, and My thoughts than your thoughts.

"For as the rain comes down, and the snow from heaven, and do not return there, but water the earth, and make it bring forth and bud, that it may give seed to the sower and bread to the eater,

So shall My word be that goes forth from My mouth; it shall not return to Me void, but it shall accomplish what I please, and it shall prosper in the thing for which I sent it.

"For you shall go out with joy, and be led out with peace; the mountains and the hills shall break forth into singing before you, and all the trees of the field shall clap their hands.

Instead of the thorn shall come up the cypress tree, and instead of the brier shall come up the myrtle tree; and it shall be to the Lord for a name, for an everlasting sign that shall not be cut off."

Isaiah 58:11 – The Lord will guide you continually, and satisfy your soul in drought, and strengthen your bones; you shall be like a watered garden, and like a spring of water, whose waters do not fail.

James 1:12 – Blessed is the man who endures temptation; for when he has been approved, he will receive the crown of life which the Lord has promised to those who love Him.

James 1:17 - Every good gift and every perfect gift is from above, and comes down from the Father of lights, with whom there is no variation or shadow of turning.

James 1:23 – For if anyone is a hearer of the word and not a doer, he is like a man observing his natural face in a mirror.

James 2:14 – What does it profit, my brethren, if someone says he has faith but does not have works? Can faith save him?

James 2:17-18 – Thus also faith by itself, if it does not have works, is dead.
But someone will say, "You have faith, and I have works." Show me your faith without your works, and I will show you my faith by my works.

James 3:17-18 - But the wisdom that is from above is first pure, then peaceable, gentle, willing to yield, full of mercy and good fruits, without partiality and without hypocrisy.
Now the fruit of righteousness is sown in peace by those who make peace.

Jeremiah 17:14 – Heal me, O Lord, and I shall be healed; save me, and I shall be saved, for You are my praise.

Jeremiah 29:11-13 – For I know the thoughts that I think toward you, says the Lord, thoughts of peace and not of evil, to give you a future and a hope.

Then you will call upon Me and go and pray to Me, and I will listen to you.

And you will seek Me and find Me, when you search for Me with all your heart.

Job 5:8-11 – "But as for me, I would seek God, and to God I would commit my cause—

Who does great things, and unsearchable, marvelous things without number.

He gives rain on the earth, and sends waters on the fields.

He sets on high those who are lowly, and those who mourn are lifted to safety."

John 3:1-6 – There was a man of the Pharisees named Nicodemus, a ruler of the Jews.

This man came to Jesus by night and said to Him, "Rabbi, we know that You are a teacher come from God; for no one can do these signs that You do unless God is with him."

Jesus answered and said to him, "Most assuredly, I say to you, unless one is born again, he cannot see the kingdom of God."

Nicodemus said to Him, "How can a man be born when he is old? Can he enter a second time into his mother's womb and be born?"

Jesus answered, "Most assuredly, I say to you, unless one is born of water and the Spirit, he cannot enter the kingdom of God.

"That which is born of the flesh is flesh, and that which is born of the Spirit is spirit."

John 5:24 – "Most assuredly, I say to you, he who hears My word and believes in Him who sent Me has everlasting life, and shall not come into judgment, but has passed from death into life."

John 8:31-32 – Then Jesus said to those Jews who believed Him, "If you abide in My word, you are My disciples indeed.

"And you shall know the truth, and the truth shall make you free."

John 10:27 – "My sheep hear My voice, and I know them, and they follow Me."

John 14:17-18 – "The Spirit of truth, whom the world cannot receive, because it neither sees Him nor knows Him; but you know Him, for He dwells with you and will be in you.

"I will not leave you orphans; I will come to you."

John 14:27-28 – "Peace I leave with you, My peace I give to you; not as the world gives do I give to you. Let not your heart be troubled, neither let it be afraid.

"You have heard Me say to you, 'I am going away and coming back to you.' If you loved Me, you would rejoice because I said, 'I am going to the Father,' for My Father is greater than I."

I John 1:5-7 – This is the message which we have heard from Him and declare to you, that God is light and in Him is no darkness at all.

If we say that we have fellowship with Him, and walk in darkness, we lie and do not practice the truth.

But if we walk in the light as He is in the light, we have fellowship with one another, and the blood of Jesus Christ His Son cleanses us from all sin.

I John 5:20 – And we know that the Son of God has come and has given us an understanding, that we may know Him who is true; and we are in Him who is true, in His Son Jesus Christ. This is the true God and eternal life.

Judges 13:20 – It happened as the flame went up toward heaven from the altar—the Angel of the Lord ascended in the flame of the altar! When Manoah and his wife saw this, they fell on their faces to the ground.

Lamentations 3:39-41 – Why should a living man complain, a man for the punishment of his sins?

Let us search out and examine our ways, and turn back to the Lord;

Let us lift our hearts and hands to God in heaven.

Luke 5:17 – Now it happened on a certain day, as He was teaching, that there were Pharisees and teachers of the law sitting by, who had come out of every town of Galilee, Judea, and Jerusalem. And the power of the Lord was present to heal them.

Luke 11:34 – "The lamp of the body is the eye. Therefore, when your eye is good, your whole body also is full of light. But when your eye is bad, your body also is full of darkness."

Luke 12:29-31 – "And do not seek what you should eat or what you should drink, nor have an anxious mind.

"For all these things the nations of the world seek after, and your Father knows that you need these things.

"But seek the kingdom of God, and all these things shall be added to you."

Luke 21:36 – "Watch therefore, and pray always that you may be counted worthy to escape all these things that will come to pass, and to stand before the Son of Man."

Luke 24:45 – And He opened their understanding, that they might comprehend the Scriptures.

Matthew 6:26 – "Look at the birds of the air, for they neither sow nor reap nor gather into barns; yet your heavenly Father feeds them. Are you not of more value than they?"

Matthew 7:12 – "Therefore, whatever you want men to do to you, do also to them, for this is the Law and the Prophets."

Matthew 22:36-40 – "Teacher, which is the great commandment in the law?"

Jesus said to him, "'You shall love the Lord your God with all your heart, with all your soul, and with all your mind.'

"This is the first and great commandment.

"And the second is like it: 'You shall love your neighbor as yourself.'

"On these two commandments hang all the Law and the Prophets."

Matthew 25:14-31 – "For the kingdom of heaven is like a man traveling to a far country, who called his own servants and delivered his goods to them.

"And to one he gave five talents, to another two, and to another one, to each according to his own ability; and immediately he went on a journey.

"Then he who had received the five talents went and traded with them, and made another five talents.

"And likewise he who had received two gained two more also.

"But he who had received one went and dug in the ground, and hid his lord's money.

"After a long time the lord of those servants came and settled accounts with them.

"So he who had received five talents came and brought five other talents, saying, 'Lord, you delivered to me five talents; look, I have gained five more talents besides them.'

"His lord said to him, 'Well done, good and faithful servant; you were faithful over a few things, I will make you ruler over many things. Enter into the joy of your lord.'

"He also who had received two talents came and said, 'Lord, you delivered to me two talents; look, I have gained two more talents besides them.'

"His lord said to him, 'Well done, good and faithful servant; you have been faithful over a few things, I will make you ruler over many things. Enter into the joy of your lord.'

"Then he who had received the one talent came and said, 'Lord, I knew you to be a hard man, reaping where you have not sown, and gathering where you have not scattered seed.

'And I was afraid, and went and hid your talent in the ground. Look, there you have what is yours.'

"But his lord answered and said to him, 'You wicked and lazy servant, you knew that I reap where I have not sown, and gather where I have not scattered seed.

'So you ought to have deposited my money with the bankers, and at my coming I would have received back my own with interest.

'Therefore take the talent from him, and give it to him who has ten talents.

'For to everyone who has, more will be given, and he will have abundance; but from him who does not have, even what he has will be taken away.

'And cast the unprofitable servant into the outer darkness. There will be weeping and gnashing of teeth.'

"When the Son of Man comes in His glory, and all the holy angels with Him, then He will sit on the throne of His glory."

Philippians 1:27 – Only let your conduct be worthy of the gospel of Christ, so that whether I come and see you or am absent, I may hear of your affairs, that you stand fast in one spirit, with one mind striving together for the faith of the gospel,

Philippians 2:1-6 – Therefore if there is any consolation in Christ, if any comfort of love, if any fellowship of the Spirit, if any affection and mercy,
Fulfill my joy by being like-minded, having the same love, being of one accord, of one mind.
Let nothing be done through selfish ambition or conceit, but in lowliness of mind let each esteem others better than himself.
Let each of you look out not only for his own interests, but also for the interests of others.
Let this mind be in you which was also in Christ Jesus,
Who, being in the form of God, did not consider it robbery to be equal with God,

Philippians 2:5 - Let this mind be in you which was also in Christ Jesus,

Philippians 4:8 – Finally, brethren, whatever things are true, whatever things are noble, whatever things are just, whatever things are pure, whatever things are lovely, whatever things are of good report, if there is any virtue and if there is anything praiseworthy—meditate on these things.

Proverbs 1:5 – A wise man will hear and increase learning, and a man of understanding will attain wise counsel,

Proverbs 3:6 – In all your ways acknowledge Him, and He shall direct your paths.

Proverbs 4:7 – Wisdom is the principal thing; therefore get wisdom. And in all your getting, get understanding.

Proverbs 4:23 – Keep your heart with all diligence, for out of it spring the issues of life.

Proverbs 5:15 – Drink water from your own cistern, and running water from your own well.

Proverbs 16:3 – Commit your works to the Lord, and your thoughts will be established.

Proverbs 17:17-18 – A friend loves at all times, and a brother is born for adversity.

A man devoid of understanding shakes hands in a pledge, and becomes surety for his friend.

Proverbs 18:2 – A fool has no delight in understanding, but in expressing his own heart.

Proverbs 22:17 – Incline your ear and hear the words of the wise, and apply your heart to my knowledge;

Psalm 1:1-3 – Blessed is the man who walks not in the counsel of the ungodly, nor stands in the path of sinners, nor sits in the seat of the scornful;

But his delight is in the law of the Lord, and in His law he meditates day and night.

He shall be like a tree planted by the rivers of water, that brings forth its fruit in its season, whose leaf also shall not wither; and whatever be does shall prosper.

Psalm 16:5 – O Lord, You are the portion of my inheritance and my cup; You maintain my lot.

Psalm 17:15 – As for me, I will see Your face in righteousness; I shall be satisfied when I awake in Your likeness.

Psalm 18:28 – For You will light my lamp; the Lord my God will enlighten my darkness.

Psalm 18:30 – As for God, His way is perfect; the word of the Lord is proven; He is a shield to all who trust in Him.

Psalm 19:7-11 – The law of the Lord is perfect, converting the soul; the testimony of the Lord is sure, making wise the simple;

The statutes of the Lord are right, rejoicing the heart; the commandment of the Lord is pure, enlightening the eyes;

The fear of the Lord is clean, enduring forever; the judgments of the Lord are true and righteous altogether.

More to be desired are they than gold, yea, than much fine gold; sweeter also than honey and the honeycomb.

Moreover by them Your servant is warned, and in keeping them there is great reward.

Psalm 36:9 – For with You is the fountain of life; in Your light we see light.

Psalm 46:1 – God is our refuge and strength, a very present help in trouble.

Psalm 51:6 – Behold, You desire truth in the inward parts, and in the hidden part You will make me to know wisdom.

Psalm 57:1 – Be merciful to me, O God, be merciful to me! For my soul trusts in You; and in the shadow of Your wings I will make my refuge, until these calamities have passed by.

Psalm 58:11 – So that men will say, "Surely there is a reward for the righteous; surely He is God who judges in the earth."

Psalm 74:17 – You have set all the borders of the earth; You have made summer and winter.

Psalm 77:13 – Your way, O God, is in the sanctuary; who is so great a God as our God?

Psalm 84:11 – For the Lord God is a sun and shield; the Lord will give grace and glory; no good thing will He withhold from those who walk uprightly.

Psalm 85:13 – Righteousness will go before Him, and shall make His footsteps our pathway.

Psalm 92:12-13 – The righteous shall flourish like a palm tree, he shall grow like a cedar in Lebanon.
Those who are planted in the house of the Lord shall flourish in the courts of our God.

Psalm 103:19 – The Lord has established His throne in heaven, and His kingdom rules over all.

Psalm 118:19 – Open to me the gates of righteousness; I will go through them, and I will praise the Lord.

Psalm 119:18 – Open my eyes, that I may see wondrous things from Your law.

Psalm 119:105 – Your word is a lamp to my feet and a light to my path.

Psalm 121 – I will lift up my eyes to the hills—from whence comes my help?
My help comes from the Lord, who made heaven and earth.
He will not allow your foot to be moved; He who keeps you will not slumber.
Behold, He who keeps Israel shall neither slumber nor sleep.
The Lord is your keeper; the Lord is your shade at your right hand.

The sun shall not strike you by day, nor the moon by night.

The Lord shall preserve you from all evil; He shall preserve your soul.

The Lord shall preserve your going out and your coming in from this time forth, and even forevermore.

Psalm 133 – Behold, how good and how pleasant it is for brethren to dwell together in unity!

It is like the precious oil upon the head, running down on the beard, the beard of Aaron, running down on the edge of his garments.

It is like the dew of Hermon, descending upon the mountains of Zion; for there the Lord commanded the blessing—life forevermore.

Revelation 3:20 – "Behold, I stand at the door and knock. If anyone hears My voice and opens the door, I will come in to him and dine with him, and he with Me."

Revelation 21:6 – And He said to me, "It is done! I am the Alpha and the Omega, the Beginning and the End. I will give of the fountain of the water of life freely to him who thirsts."

Revelation 22:1-5 – And he showed me a pure river of water of life, clear as crystal, proceeding from the throne of God and of the Lamb.

In the middle of its street, and on either side of the river, was the tree of life, which bore twelve fruits, each tree yielding its fruit every month. The leaves of tree were for the healing of the nations.

And there shall be no more curse, but the throne of God and of the Lamb shall be in it, and His servants shall serve Him.

They shall see His face, and His name shall be on their foreheads.

There shall be no night there: they need no lamp nor light of the sun, for the Lord God gives them light. And they shall reign forever and ever.

Revelation 22:16 – "I, Jesus, have sent My angel to testify to you these things in the churches. I am the Root and the Offspring of David, the Bright and Morning Star."

Romans 2:7 – Eternal life to those who by patient continuance in doing good seek for glory, honor, and immortality;

Romans 8:2 – For the law of the Spirit of life in Christ Jesus has made me free from the law of sin and death.

Romans 8:16 – The Spirit Himself bears witness with our spirit that we are children of God,

Romans 8:28 – And we know that all things work together for good to those who love God, to those who are the called according to His purpose.

Romans 12:2 – And do not be conformed to this world, but be transformed by the renewing of your mind, that you may prove what is that good and acceptable and perfect will of God.

II Samuel 22:33 – God is my strength and power, and He makes my way perfect.

Song of Solomon 2:11 – For lo, the winter is past, the rain is over and gone.

Song of Solomon 2:12 – The flowers appear on the earth; the time of singing has come, and the voice of the turtledove is heard in our land.

I Thessalonians 3:8 – For now we live, if you stand fast in the Lord.

I Thessalonians 4:4 – That each of you should know how to possess his own vessel in sanctification and honor,

I Thessalonians 5:23 – Now may the God of peace Himself sanctify you completely; and may your whole spirit, soul, and body be preserved blameless at the coming of our Lord Jesus Christ.

II Thessalonians 1:3 – We are bound to thank God always for you, brethren, as it is fitting, because your faith grows exceedingly, and the love of every one of you all abounds toward each other,

II Thessalonians 3:5 – Now may the Lord direct your hearts into the love of God and into the patience of Christ.

II Thessalonians 3:10 – For even when we were with you, we commanded you this; if anyone will not work, neither shall he eat.

II Timothy 1:7 – For God has not given us a spirit of fear, but of power and of love and of a sound mind.

II Timothy 2:18-19 – Who have strayed concerning the truth, saying that the resurrection is already past; and they overthrow the faith of some.

Nevertheless the solid foundation of God stands, having this seal: "The Lord knows those who are His," and, "Let everyone who names the name of Christ depart from iniquity."

II Timothy 3:15 – And that from childhood you have known the Holy Scriptures, which are able to make you wise for salvation through faith which is in Christ Jesus.

Titus 1:2 – In hope of eternal life which God, who cannot lie, promised before time began,

Zechariah 8:12 – 'For the seed shall be prosperous, the vine shall give its fruit, the ground shall give her increase, and the heavens shall give their dew— I will cause the remnant of this people to possess all these.'

Veni Creator Spiritus
Mentes tuorum visita
Imple superna gratia
Quæ tu creasti pectora
Accende lumen sensibus
Fantes tuorum visita
Confirma nostri corporis
Virtute firmans perpetim

CHISEL CARVING TRANSLATION

Come, Holy Ghost, Creator blest,
and in our hearts take up Thy rest;
come with Thy grace and heav'nly aid,
To fill the hearts which Thou hast made.

Thy light to every sense impart,
and in our hearts take up Thy rest;
thine own unfailing might supply
to strengthen our infirmity.

English translation of: Veni Creator Spiritus: Come, Holy Ghost. Retrieved November 30, 2006, from http://www.chantcd.com/lyrics/come_holy_ghost.ht

INDEX TO THE WRITINGS OF ELEANOR
STREICHER FABER

A
Acceptance, 13
Acquiescence, 14
Affirmation, 15
Angels Wings, 16
Apple, An, 17
Attraction, 18

B
Balance, 19
Be Flexible, 20
Beacon, The, 21
Behind Closed Doors, 22
Bondage, 23
Bow and Arrow, 24

C
Caboose, 25
Casket—Basket, 26
Castle, The, 27
Cellar of Escape, 28
Center of Life, 29
Child of God, 30
Children, 31
Chisel, 32
Chisel Carving
    Translation, 167
Closing, 139
Comforter, 33
Creative, 34
Creative Spirit, 35
Creator, 36

D
Deception, 37
Demonstrate, 38
Desert of Life, 39
Divine Mind, 40
Door, The, 41

F
Faith, 42
Father of Lights, 43
Feelings, 44
Fool, The, 45
Fragile, 46
Freedom, 47
Furnace of Life, 48
Future, 49

G
Garden of Choice, 50
Gates, 51
Generator, 52
Genesis, 53
God, 54
God Ideas, 55
God is All, 139
God is My Light, 56
God's Child, 57
God's Sanctuary, 58
Golden Rule—Creative
    Love, 59

H
Hall of Justice, 60
Harden Not Your Heart,
    61
Heart of Flesh, 62
Holy Spirit, 63
House or Home, 64

I
I Am a Child of God, 65
Impress—Express, 66
In Closing, 139
In Memory, 67
Indian Chief, 68
Internal Flame, 69
Intuition, 70

K
Karma, 71
Katie on the Wrong Track,
    72
Know Thyself, 73

L
Life is a Parity, 74
Love, 75

M
Magical Power, 76
Mind Over Matter, 77
My Body, 78
Myself, 79

N
Name of Love, 80
New Creation, 81
Notice, 82

O
Oneness with God, 83
Open—Alive—Alert, 84
Opening Prayer, 11-12

P
Peace and Sunshine, 85
Peace of God, The, 86
Pebble Represents
    Growth, 87
Pebbles Order Form, 176
Pilot of Your Vessel, 88
Platform, 90-91
Positivity, 89
Prayer, 92
Praying, 93

R
Rainbow, 94
Reaction, 95
Reflection, 96
Remain Open, 97
Replace, 98
Replenish, 99
Replica, 100
Resource, 101
Right Thinking, 102
Righteousness, 103
River Stone, 104
Rose or Carnation, 105
Ruffled Feathers, 106

S
Seeds, 107
Self, 108
Self-Deception, 109
Self-Evaluation, 110
Self-Projection, 111
Sensibility—Sensitivity, 112
Sensitivity, 113
Silence, 114
Sincerity, 115
Something Told Me, 116
Soul Discovery, 117
Soul Growth, 118
Spark of Life, 119
Spectator and Director, 120
Spirit of Truth, 121
Step Aside, 122
Success, 123
Success: Chance or Choice, 124
Summer, 125

T
Tandem, 126
Temple of God, 127
Thoughts, 128
Three Drops of Blood, 129
Torch of Love, 130
Trust and Believe, 131

U
Unified Four, 132

W
Winter, 133
Wisdom, 134
Within, 135
Work, 136

Y
You Are God's Diamond, 137
Your Concealed Being, 138

INDEX TO SCRIPTURE REFERENCES

Acts 14:22, 71, 143

II Chronicles 31:21, 80, 143

Colossians 2:2-3, 130, 143

I Corinthians 2:10, 63, 143
I Corinthians 3:1-3, 105, 143
I Corinthians 3:7-10, 116, 144
I Corinthians 3:13-14, 66, 144
I Corinthians 6:19, 127, 144
I Corinthians 12:6, 82, 144
I Corinthians 14:40, 132, 144

II Corinthians 4:15-18, 117, 145
II Corinthians 5:1-8, 64, 145
II Corinthians 8:21, 79, 146
II Corinthians 12:14, 31, 146

Deuteronomy 3:24, 136, 146

Deuteronomy 4:4, 54, 146
Deuteronomy 4:20, 48, 146

Ephesians 2:10, 34, 146
Ephesians 2:20-22, 113, 146
Ephesians 6:24, 115, 147

Exodus 3:14, 65, 147
Exodus 20:1-3, 29, 147

Ezekiel 11:19-20, 15, 44, 147
Ezekiel 36:26, 62, 147

Galatians 6:7-9, 19, 148

Genesis 1:26-27, 36, 148

Hebrews 11:1, 20, 148

Hosea 14:5, 46, 148

Isaiah 9:6, 133, 148
Isaiah 55:6-13, 107, 148
Isaiah 58:11, 50, 149

James 1:12, 60, 149
James 1:17, 43, 150
James 1:23, 96, 150
James 2:14, 93, 150
James 2:17-18, 38, 150

James 3:17-18, 32, 103, 150

Jeremiah 17:14, 102, 150
Jeremiah 29:11-13, 39, 151

Job 5:8-11, 108, 151

John 3:1-6, 83, 151
John 5:24, 74, 152
John 8:31-32, 22, 152
John 10:27, 124, 152
John 14:17-18, 33, 152
John 14:27-28, 86, 152

I John 1:5-7, 21, 52, 55, 152
I John 5:20, 14, 153

Judges 13:20, 69, 153

Lamentations 3:39-41, 109, 153

Luke 5:17, 77, 153
Luke 11:34, 78, 154
Luke 12:29-31, 101, 154
Luke 21:36, 28, 154
Luke 24:45, 97, 154

Matthew 6:26, 13, 154
Matthew 7:12, 59, 154
Matthew 22:36-40, 75, 155
Matthew 25:14-31, 81, 155

Philippians 1:27, 138, 156
Philippians 2:1-6, 110, 157
Philippians 2:5, 40, 114, 157
Philippians 4:8, 73, 157

Proverbs 1:5, 128, 157
Proverbs 3:6, 120, 157
Proverbs 4:7, 134, 158
Proverbs 4:23, 27, 158
Proverbs 5:15, 68, 158
Proverbs 16:3, 25, 158
Proverbs 17:17-18, 118, 158
Proverbs 18:2, 45, 158
Proverbs 22:17, 41, 158

Psalm 1:1-3, 99, 119, 158
Psalm 16:5, 57, 90, 159
Psalm 17:15, 61, 100, 159
Psalm 18:28, 56, 159
Psalm 18:30, 53, 121, 159
Psalm 19:7-11, 106, 159
Psalm 36:9, 104, 111, 160
Psalm 46:1, 135, 160
Psalm 51:6, 70, 160
Psalm 57:1, 16, 160
Psalm 58:11, 92, 160
Psalm 74:17, 125, 160
Psalm 77:13, 58, 160
Psalm 84:11, 94, 160
Psalm 85:13, 122, 161
Psalm 92:12-13, 26, 161
Psalm 103:19, 131, 161
Psalm 118:19, 51, 161
Psalm 119:18, 97, 161

Psalm 119:105, 88, 161
Psalm 121, 98, 161
Psalm 133, 84, 162

Revelation 3:20, 41, 162
Revelation 7:14, 129
Revelation 21:6, 47, 162
Revelation 22:1-5, 112, 162
Revelation 22:16, 87, 137, 163

Romans 2:7, 67, 163
Romans 8:2, 23, 163
Romans 8:16, 57, 163
Romans 8:17, 129
Romans 8:28, 126, 163
Romans 12:2, 95, 164

II Samuel 22:33, 18, 164

Song of Solomon 2:11, 49, 164
Song of Solomon 2:12, 76, 164

I Thessalonians 3:8, 89, 164
I Thessalonians 4:4, 24, 164
I Thessalonians 5:23, 85, 164

II Thessalonians 1:3, 42, 165
II Thessalonians 3:5, 123, 165
II Thessalonians 3:10, 35, 165

II Timothy 1:7, 76, 165
II Timothy 2:18-19, 37, 72, 165
II Timothy 3:15, 30, 165

Titus 1:2, 105, 165

Zechariah 8:12, 17, 166

PEBBLES ORDER FORM

Additional copies of *PEBBLES: Poems and Writings of Spiritual Inspiration* by Eleanor Streicher Faber are available through Aaron Press for $14.95 each, plus $3.00 shipping and handling.

Please send:

1 copy of *Pebbles* $17.95

Additional copies add $14.95 each.......... $_____

Total enclosed .... $_____

Name: _____

Address: _____

City: _____

State: _____ Zip: _____

Phone: _____

Email: _____

Send a check or money order payable to Aaron Press to:

AARON PRESS
PO BOX 164
NAPERVILLE, IL 60566-0164